Are
N

ROCK YOUR NETWORK®
FOR JOB
SEEKERS

How to Rebuild Your Network in 5 Minutes
a Day Online and Off

by Networking Coach
Wendy Terwelp

OPPORTUNITY KNOCKS™

11431 N. Port Washington Rd., Suite 101, Mequon, WI 53092
800.969.KNOX | consultant@knocks.com | www.knocks.com

Rock Your Network® for Job Seekers: How to Rebuild Your Network in 5 Minutes a Day Online and Off

ISBN: 978-0-578-03129-3

Requests to the author for permission should be addressed to:

Opportunity Knocks
11431 N. Port Washington Rd., Ste. 101
Mequon, WI 53092
Phone: 262.241.4655
Fax: 262.241.4679

Limit of Liability/Disclaimer of Warranty: While the author has used her best efforts in preparing this book, she makes no representations or warranties with respect to the accuracy or completeness of the contents of this book and specifically disclaims any implied warranties or merchantability or fitness for a particular purpose. No warrants may be created or extended by sales representatives or written sales materials. The advice and strategies contained herein may not be suitable for your situation. Consult with a professional where appropriate. The author shall not be liable for readers' ability to secure employment. Readers understand a commitment of time and action on their part is optimal in order to see results. The author shall not be liable for any loss of profit or any other commercial damages, including but not limited to special, incidental, consequential or other damages.

Please note, while all the stories and anecdotes described in this book are based on true experiences, most of the names are pseudonyms and some situations have been changed slightly for educational purposes and to protect each individual's privacy.

CONTENTS

ABOUT THE AUTHOR

Wendy J. Terwelp has helped thousands of clients get hired faster and be rock stars at work since 1989. A recognized expert on networking, both online and off, Wendy has been featured in *The Wall Street Journal*, *The Washington Post*, *The Chicago Tribune*, *The Philadelphia Inquirer*, *Fast Company*, *The Business Journal*, Monster.com, Careerbuilder.com, and more as well as numerous radio shows. She has published hundreds of articles on the web and in print.

Wendy has a huge network and has been razzed about networking throughout her life. She decided to use this to her advantage and write this book to help others turn networking pain to career gain.

According to her mom, one-year-old Wendy walked up to strangers and said, "Hi," while smiling and waving wildly.

Years later, she became known for her ability to remember names and something unique about the people she meets. This ability, along with the tips provided in this book, help Wendy maintain connections throughout her life and work. She is still friends with former bosses, clients, colleagues, and coworkers as well as friends from grade school, high school, and college.

ACKNOWLEDGMENTS

People rock! Thank you to all who have been in my network and my life. Thanks also to those entering it now by reading this book. Without you, this book would not be possible.

I would especially like to thank my family, friends, clients, and colleagues for their encouragement and willingness to share some of their cool stories and experiences.

Thanks to my Review Team who patiently reviewed every line and provided terrific feedback. If you spot an error, it's mine, not theirs.

Special thanks to my family: Kris Terwelp, Mike Terwelp, and Julie Terwelp along with my parents, Rose and Mike. Thanks to Julie Terwelp, SnapHappy Creative, LLC, who designed all the rock star graphics. Thanks also to Jennifer Alcorn for her persistent prodding.

CHAPTER 1
GET READY TO
ROCK YOUR NETWORK!

Got no time? You're not alone. That's the biggest complaint I hear from job seekers and the currently employed when we talk about networking. But, who says networking has to be a two-hour lunch meeting?

Here's a secret, you can rebuild your network using just five minutes a day!

Whether you're a job seeker or a currently employed careerist, building and maintaining your network is essential to having it there for you when you need it.

Looking for a job? Reconnect with your network and help them, even though you are the one in need. (Check out Bob, The Likable Engineer's story on page 42!)

Currently employed? Build an internal network to help you snag your next promotion. (Learn how Steve snagged his gigs and promotions by staying in touch on page 65.)

It's not what you know; it's who you know that gets you hired. We've all heard this phrase so many times our ears are bleeding, right?

Here are the facts:

66% to 85% of people land new careers through networking.

Networking is 10 times more effective than posting your resume online or answering job ads. When you think about this, where should you spend the most of your job search time?

If you said networking — get ready to rock your network and get hired faster!

I can't wait to hear about your results.

-Wendy

It's not what you know; it's who you know that gets you hired.

CHAPTER 2
WHY NETWORK?

Think about it this way, how many people have you helped in your life? Yes, helping your pals move counts. Time for them to help you.

When I work with job seekers, even at the most senior levels, they shudder at the word "networking." They forget that networking is helping and that they have helped many people throughout their work and life.

Job seekers tell me networking is more work than net and that networking means long meetings, long lunches, and networking events that are a waste of time. One executive told me, "I never gave it much thought while I was working. I know a lot of people. However, networking seems so uncomfortable to me... It almost appears as though you're intruding on productive time."

Having a solid network is especially critical in tough economic times. For example, one recruiter told me he looks at 200 to 300 resumes a day, seven days a week. With this type of volume, it's important to tap your network. You can then learn about opportunities **before** they hit the want ads.

> One recruiter told me he looks at 200 to 300 resumes a day, seven days a week.

In order to get the most from your network, you want your network to be there when you need it, which means you've got to maintain it. In this book, I provide tons of tips, tricks, and strategies to help you rebuild your network in five minutes a day.

THE STATS

According to Gerry Crispin & Mark Mehler's CareerXroads' 2009 Source of Hire Study, **Internal Transfers and Promotions were 38.8% of ALL the full-time positions a company fills.**

> **Rock Star Tip:** What does this mean for you? If you're currently employed, build an internal network of colleagues, managers, and staff from other departments so you can reap the rewards and get that promotion.

The study showed **referrals make up 27.3% of all external hires** and is arguably the No. 1 one external source. Referral sources include employees, alumni, vendors, etc.

Rock Star Tip: In Chapter 3, I cover your circle of influence, who's all in it, and how to think BIG. You'll want to reconnect with all the people in your network, because referrals are the No. 1 source for hiring external candidates.

According to the study, **Job Boards represent 12.3% of external hires**. These statistics represent job board companies like Monster and CareerBuilder and do not include career pages within a company's website.

Rock Star Tip: While job boards do yield results, I consider them the "spray and pray" method of job hunting. By this I mean candidates spray resumes all over the internet and pray someone calls them. Yes, you can use a job board — but take it to the next level. Do you know someone who knows an employee of the company posting the job opening? You do? Contact them FIRST.

 # FRIEDA'S STORY

Frieda discovered she loved a company where she had interned while earning her latest certification. She wanted to snag a permanent role with this organization. Knowing that internal transfers and promotions are 38.8% of ALL the full-time positions a company fills,

Frieda got names from inside her company and built an internal network. She writes:

"Wendy is a firm believer in networking. For me, this was the most difficult change in how I do things. In the past, I would look at job ads as my first source for openings. This time I talked to anyone who knew anyone in coding and who they report to. I got names. … I sent my cover letter and resume directly to the decision makers thereby bypassing HR [human resources]. I received a call very soon and it was for a position that I would not have ordinarily applied for because the qualifications seemed so much more extensive than what I had."

Frieda was offered the position at a salary that was 68% more than she was making in her previous role.

COACHING CHALLENGE

When reviewing the CareerXroads findings, think about how you are currently spending your job search time. What percentage are you putting into networking versus responding to online ads ("spraying and praying")? Is it time to rethink your strategy? Use the CareerXRoads stats, **66.1% stated source of hires were from networking**, to determine how you spend your time. Get names and set up some networking meetings. It worked for my client Frieda; it can work for you.

PLAY LIST ▸▸ TAKE ACTION!

☒

01. Knowing that 66.1% of job seekers land gigs through their network (internal and external), I have taken a long hard look at how I am spending my job search time.

02. To use my job hunting time wisely, I resolved to make at least five reconnections to people in my network this week.

03. I created a job search plan and reallocated my time with a greater focus on networking.

04. I read Chapter 7 for more ideas to help me build and retain my network using the **ONE SECRET** that ensures my network is there for me when I need it. I will fuel my network to fire it up.

CHAPTER 3
YOUR CIRCLE OF INFLUENCE: THINK BIG

When I work with clients on identifying the people in their network, we work on thinking BIG when listing who they know. Why? Sometimes job seekers get stuck in a rut, thinking that the only people who can help them are people in the same field holding similar positions. Not true!

 ## LISA'S STORY

Lisa was a teacher who was tired of her current school district and wanted to relocate to one closer to her home.

To do so, Lisa networked with all her teacher friends. She told me they had no contacts in her preferred school district and did not know of any job openings.

"Think BIG," I told her. "Let's make a list of every single person you know."

"But, they're not all teachers," she replied.

That's not the point of course.

I don't know about you, but I know a lot more people who do things other than career coaching or personal branding (my field). I know all kinds of terrific people, and I'm sure you do too.

Lisa diligently expanded her list of contacts and created a new sound bite she could use to network more effectively. (Learn how to create your own sound bite in Chapter 5.)

She decided to try it out with the handyman working in her home. After learning more about her work experience, the handyman ran to his car, came back with a cell phone, and said, "Here. My daughter is the human resources director for that school district and she's on the line."

Lisa landed an interview with her first choice school district for the following week.

Lisa thought big. Now it's your turn. The first part of reconnecting and rebuilding your network is making a list of all the people who are in your circle of influence — your network.

I think you'll be surprised, when you develop and expand your list of people in your network. You know a lot of people and so do they. Remember the Source of Hire study in Chapter 1? If you combine internal networks with external ones, 66.1 percent of people land jobs through people they know (their network).

Other surveys showed that more than 70 percent of all jobs are found through networking. And with many jobs not being advertised (remember those internal networks inside companies), it's important to build and maintain your contact list. With that in mind, here is a list of the types of people you may know. Time to build your own list! Think BIG.

THE "THINK BIG" NETWORK LIST

Industry providers

Who buys from your company and who does your company buy from? These contacts can lead to unadvertised openings with your company's clients or vendors.

Co-workers - past and present

Be sure you know who will and who won't keep your confidence.

 ## CHRIS' STORY

Chris got laid off, but never lost ties with his former employer. He told me, "Thankfully I did not burn any bridges when I left and after being off for a month, I landed back (with my former employer) as the Prospect Sales Manager. Crazy how things work out, but thankfully they have."

Your clients

List all of them and their current information. Staying in touch with clients can lead to some fantastic gigs, including a new job, speaking events, invitations to professional organizations, networking events, business contacts, and more because you took the time to stay in touch.

 ## TINA'S STORY

Tina landed a terrific unadvertised position as a controller.

She said, "I just started contacting my clients discreetly. One of them passed my resume along to a company president on a Saturday. I got a call at 10 a.m. the same day! After four interviews, I was hired."

Because she had such high recommendations from her own clients within her network, she also won a 17 percent raise, performance bonus after 60 days, and a clothing allowance.

Service providers

Who do you buy personal services from? Think big. On your list, include people you see only once a year or infrequently such as hairdressers, dentists, massage therapists, attorneys, homebuilders, physicians, lawn services, etc. These service providers have many clients and many connections in your local area.

Family members

List extended family members in addition to immediate family members. Yes, the third-cousin-twice-removed may know someone you need to know. I could go on and on here because I am fortunate enough to have great people in my family who helped me produce this book. The graphic designer for my website and this book happens to be my sister-in-law. My sister is an English professor and my brother is an engineer whose expertise is in the details.

And, if you're a student looking for your first job, don't forget your parents.

 ## WENDY'S STORY

When I was in college deciding if I truly wanted to remain an art major, I talked to my dad who introduced me to a friend of his from church. This friend, Mr. S., was a vice president at a large printing firm in the area, which had its own art department. I called him up and referenced my dad. He told me, "Come and take a tour. I'll introduce you to the head of the art department."

Can you believe it? I had an informational interview and I didn't even know what one was! To get the most from this meeting, I wanted to be prepared, so I created a set of questions to ask the art director. Mr. S. personally introduced me to the director after the tour. The art director answered all my questions and introduced me to some of the artists. They were very talented and willing to answer my questions too.

Then the art director said, "You know kid, you have guts. I like you. I'm going to connect you with some ad agencies in town. They have a different environment than an art department. This will give you a good picture of the different types of careers for art majors."

Cool! I then met and talked with all the major firms in the area. After all of the meetings and interviews, I reviewed the notes I had taken, compared them with my qualifications, and decided to change majors. I later earned a degree in Mass Communication / Journalism. In talking with all those art directors, I learned how to interview well and applied what I learned immediately.

Talking with decision-makers and learning about their businesses and professions is a skill set I carried throughout my career and have recommended to my job seeking clients. One client used this technique and landed a great position in advertising as a result. Her mom knew a radio personality who knew an ad person, which led to a meeting and an offer.

Professional organizations and trade groups

Professional organizations like the Public Relations Society of America (PRSA) for public relations professionals and other professional organizations often have members-only job postings. If you're a member, you get access. In addition, meeting members in person during events can pay off.

 ELSIE'S STORY

Elsie, a newspaper reporter, wanted to make a career change. She said, "One phone call to someone I've been acquainted with through the newspaper business led me to obtaining a newsletter that posted jobs listings for public relations positions biweekly. The woman I called turned out to be an officer in the local chapter of the PRSA. (It's amazing how many connections you have without realizing it!)

Elsie used this strategy to change careers and land a new job.

Volunteer organizations

Not only yours, but your kids' too — including Boy Scouts, Girl Scouts, Church, Rotary, Lion's Club, Chamber of Commerce, PTA, etc. List them all and their members. You never know; talking with a parent while organizing the Girl Scouts' cookie drive can win an interview for an unadvertised position.

 KIM'S STORY

Kim, an MBA with an information technology background, had recently relocated. She told me she knew no one in town and had no network. I recommended that she volunteer for her local chamber of commerce and that she take an active role.

Not only did Kim join the chamber, she volunteered to revamp the chamber's outdated website. Doing so gave her the opportunity to connect with every business member in the chamber to update their profiles and contacts listed on the website.

Business owners were impressed with Kim's work and one connection during this project led to an interview. Kim nailed the interview and landed the job.

Personal sports teams and your kids' teams.

Use the time spent on the sidelines or on the bench to your advantage and network. (See Chapter 5 to create a networking sound bite you can use everywhere.) Also, expand your idea of sports — bowling teams and chess clubs count here. Networking during these events can help you win more than a game; you could win a job interview!

 ## MOLLY'S STORY

Molly was out of work for 18 months and told me, "If you tell me I have to network, I'm going to scream!" She said she had already been networking with every person she knew. She asked them, "Do you know anyone who's hiring?" Not an effective strategy.

Together, Molly and I revamped her communication style to a focused, benefit-laden sound bite. She used it during her next bowling league event. Now her teammates knew what she did, the benefit she could bring to an employer, and where she wanted to work. One teammate's son was able to help her land an interview with her first-choice employer.

Molly's bowling league paid off. She got the job.

Alumni — past, present, and future

Who doesn't want to help a fellow alumnus, sorority sister or fraternity brother? You both went to the same school and know the quality of the programs and degrees earned from the school. This makes alumni even more willing to help.

 ## JONATHAN'S STORY

Jonathan was ready to make a move. His idea: use his college alumni to expand his network. I thought this was an excellent idea and looked forward to hearing about his results.

Jonathan took action and called me after landing his new gig. He told me about his results using his alumni network. "I went 10 years behind my graduation date, and 10 years in front of it. All of the alumni were glad to help out a fellow alumnus. This led to getting contacts right inside the company, which led to me landing a gig. And we all still keep in touch," he said.

Jonathan has already been promoted several times by staying connected with his network.

COACHING CHALLENGE

My challenge for you, use the above ideas to expand your network and take it even further. Here are some suggestions:

- Review and add/delete from your current networking contact database. Expand your horizons beyond your own industries and traditional contacts using some of the ideas in this chapter. Want more help creating your list? Check out our customized list-building worksheets on page 81.

- Now that you've made your list, ask yourself "Who do I know who can help me get the job of my dreams?" Then create a sound bite that lets people know what type of career you want, what you bring to the table, and where you'd like to work. This helps them help you best. Learn more about creating your own sound bite in Chapter 5.

- Don't forget about that pile of business cards on your desk. Scan in or enter a few per day into your contact management system to whittle down the pile. If you can't remember who someone is on the card, they're no longer a viable resource for your network. Throw out the card.

- To help you avoid piles of unknown people's business cards in the future, next time you're at an event and get a card, jot down the name of the event and date on the back of the card. Then jot down something unique about this person you learned during the event. This will help you recall that person in the future.

PLAY LIST ▶▶TAKE ACTION! ☒

01.   I made my list and I thought BIG.

02.   I reconnected with five people this week.

03.   I scanned in the business cards
       on my desk and tossed out the
       ones I didn't recognize.

04.   I updated my contact management
       system with the latest information,
       including where people work
       and their relationship to me.

CHAPTER 4
KNOW YOUR BRAND

ROCK YOUR CAREER®

The legendary rock band *The Who* posed the immortal question: "Who Are You?" They aren't the only ones who want to know. Potential employers will ask you the same thing, and you need to be ready with an answer that makes you look good and stand out from the crowd.

In order to know what to say to get the best results, it's important to know who you are, what you stand for, and why people should hire you. This makes it much easier for people to help you. To help you get a better understanding of your brand and what makes you stand out, ask yourself the following questions:

- What makes me a star? Translation for employers: Why should I hire you?

- What differentiates me from all other job seekers?

- What transferable skills do I bring to the table that no one else offers?

- What are my four core values I can't live without?

- What are my top five achievements of all time? What are the skills, abilities, and values used to achieve them? What's the common thread running through each?

- What is my vision for the world?

- If I could do anything — no limits — what would it be?

Answering these and similar questions can help you identify your personal brand. By knowing who you are, what you want, and what makes you unique, you will be able to clearly communicate your goals and unique value to people in your network and to potential employers.

 ## LAURA'S STORY

Laura was in a high-level management role, and when the company was bought out, she lost her job. We worked together on identifying her values, purpose, passion, and vision for the world. This is key to helping people understand what they want — and how they can use their talents for their next big gig.

Through our work together, Laura realized she did not want to work for another manufacturer. She wanted to work for the government and make a positive contribution. She identified her talents and unique value proposition. Together, we created a dynamic resume that conveyed her value and transferable skills — using the format required by government positions.

Next, Laura used her network and her sound research skills to identify positions that were a close match to her unique value and talents. With persistence and solid follow through, Laura landed a top government position, moved to Washington DC, and within a year, earned a promotion.

This is what knowing your brand and effectively conveying your value to others can do for you.

Like Laura, knowing your personal brand will help you network without begging because you will be focused. You know what you want, the types of places you wish to work — and the places you don't. You know what type of people you enjoy working with — and those you don't. Good brands take a stand.

COACHING CHALLENGE

■ Do you know how other people perceive you? If not, take a survey. Ask friends, family, colleagues, coworkers, managers and others whom you trust what they think your top five skills are and the top three words that come to mind when they think of you.

- Want more help? Take the 360Reach personal brand assessment. This assessment is focused on the positive and used as a developmental tool. Learn more about this assessment and personal branding at www.knocks.com/RockCareer/CareerBrand.html.

PLAY LIST ▸▸ TAKE ACTION!

⊠

01. I am confident in myself and my abilities and I know what I want.

02. I have a solid brand statement that clearly communicates my rock star qualities.

03. I am clear about my values and passions.

04. I know my vision and purpose.

05. I weigh my options and offers to see if they are a fit for my brand.

CHAPTER 5
CREATE A NETWORKING SOUND BITE

Every time I help my clients create a dynamic sound bite, I hear The Rolling Stones singing, "Please allow me to introduce myself…" in my head.

I can sing the whole song because Mick Jagger and Keith Richards created a memorable character with solid lyrics and an introduction that told people who the character was, what he's done, and why you should guess his name.

Only rock stars like Mick and Keith can create lyrics like those in "Sympathy for the Devil," but you can create a sound bite that is right for you, your brand, and your career search.

Creating a dynamic sound bite, like great song lyrics, is something people easily remember and can repeat to others in their network. Your sound bite is a tool you can use (and reuse) in all of your communications — emails, letters, phone conversations, events, meetings, etc.

A great sound bite, like song lyrics, is easy to remember and repeat.

ROCK YOUR NETWORK®
THREE-STEP SYSTEM

How do you create a strong sound bite for yourself? Here are the steps to create your script:

1. **FOCUS:** Be specific about what you want. Name the position title. For example, "Public Relations Consultant."

2. **SHARE:** Share what you are most proud of, one of your recent accomplishments. Think about it as a benefit statement. What skill or talent do you bring to the table that would make an employer say, "Wow, I need to hire this person!"

   Example: *"I wrote and executed a strategic crisis communications plan for a multi-billion dollar pharmaceutical company. This plan outlined decision points and provided a basis for monitoring emerging issues and trends which could have a detrimental impact on the industry."*

3. **TELL:** Tell your network where you'd like to work; name the companies.

   Example: *"I'd like to work for Merck, Roche, or GlaxoSmithKline. Who do you know who knows someone at one of these three firms?"*

MOLLY'S SOUND BITE

In Chapter 3, you learned about Molly, her hatred of networking, and how she revamped her verbal and written communications to help her network more effectively. Here's her full story and how she used her new sound bite to land her next big gig:

> Molly was a star programmer/analyst. She was so top notch that she ran all the IT projects for her company including coordinating with other departments and providing staff training on the new systems.
>
> Unfortunately, Molly was downsized when her company was acquired and was out of work for more than a year before coming to me for help. "I asked everyone for a job," she said. "I sent out an email to everyone and everything."
>
> The email read something like this, "Hi Everyone, I just got downsized and need a job. Know anyone who's hiring?"
>
> Even if her friends wanted to help her, they could not. She did not tell them what type of position she was looking for, what companies she was targeting or what skills/achievements she could bring to the table.
>
> In addition to revamping Molly's resume to focus and support her new career target, project management, we worked together to

think big and broaden her network (it's not just who you know, but who they know, and who needs to know about you). Using the sound bite strategy outlined above — Focus, Share Tell — we revamped her verbal and written communications. Notice that we also included a nice reference from her last performance review.

Her new email, which she sent to her network connections, looked like this:

Subject: News Update from Molly!

Hi Everyone,

I've been working with a career coach to help me get to the next level in my job search — i.e. employment!

I am looking for a project management position with any of the following five companies: Digital Gurus, AMCO, Giant Software, Internet Global or SoftwareXpress. Do any of you know anyone at these companies who can provide me with more information on the companies' management style, software systems or other relevant information?

I have done some research on my own through The Business Journal and the Internet, but would love the inside scoop. Lunch is on me, by the way, if we can set up a meeting.

For those of you who only know my bowling average, I'd like to share a little information about my most recent project. This will help you better understand what I have to offer a potential employer:

In my most recent role, I directed and performed installation of [software] releases, consistently under IBM's end-of-service due dates. Projects included researching and ordering software and hardware and installing, testing, and implementing software releases, with zero downtime to production. I also trained a staff of 20 in release changes and new procedures.

Because of my efforts on this project (and others), my IT Director said in a recent review: "On all system software products, Molly keeps versions current and is in complete control of testing and implementing new updates. Her thorough testing process has made her implementation record very successful. She is an extremely productive employee who is prompt in completing assignments."

I'm really excited about getting back out there and would love to talk with anyone you know who might have some ideas for me.

Thanks so much for your help! If you or any of your contacts need a copy of my resume forwarded, please let me know. I will do so immediately upon request.

Sincerely,

Molly

In less than three weeks of completing our one-month program, Molly was hired by one of her target companies. This company employed the son of a friend from her bowling league. Before this new email and communications package, her friend had no idea what Molly really did — until now.

COACHING CHALLENGE

After my presentation at a purchasing association meeting, one woman said to me, "No wonder! I kept asking people if they needed a great purchasing agent. That's begging!" Actually it's only missing two points — a benefit statement to share with her network and company names of where she wants to work.

What have you been saying while networking? If your pitch sounds more like, "Know anyone who's hiring?" and less like Molly's focused sound bite, revamp yours and try it out.

Your turn! Let us know what happens!

REMEMBER TO USE THE ROCK YOUR NETWORK® THREE-STEP SYSTEM

Focus ■ Share ■ Tell

PLAY LIST ▸▸ TAKE ACTION!

[X]

01. I've reviewed and revamped my sound bite.

02. I tested it out on my friends, family, and former coworkers.

03. I turned it into an email and sent it to _____ people this week.

04. I tried my new sound bite at a professional networking event.

05. I track the people with whom I share my sound bite so I can follow up.

CHAPTER 6
ROCK STAR NETWORKING BASICS

You know you've got to network – that's why you bought this book and worked so hard on your circle of influence list in Chapter 3 and your sound bite in Chapter 5. But sometimes just thinking about networking can be paralyzing. With this in mind, start small! Start in your comfort zone – family, friends, former colleagues, and others whom you trust. They're in the list you created in Chapter 3. Remember the basics when you reconnect.

ROCK STAR NETWORKING TIPS

Build relationships.

Networking is not a one-time transaction — networking is a two-way street. Build ties with your new contacts. By helping them get what they want, you'll get what you want. You've got to fuel your network to fire it up. This is the best way to ensure your network is there for you when you need it.

NETWORKING HORROR STORY

A friend of mine went to a networking event and shared this horror story:

She said, "I struck up a conversation with an event 'ambassador' who sold makeup products. When I said I loved the products and already had a rep, the woman gave me back my business card and said, 'Well, I guess I won't be needing this!' and walked away. Some ambassador!"

The problem with thinking about making a sale (or landing a job) with every connection is that this "ambassador" did not realize my friend had six sisters and a host of other people who may have been terrific clients for this person's makeup products. Networking is a two-way street.

Always asking for favors kills the network.

For example, at one networking event I attended, a business owner talked only about what she wanted from the group and what she sold during the entire event. Not once did she ask someone at our table what they did or how she could help them. Not surprisingly, she is no longer in business.

Smile.

Smiling controls the release of the enzyme that causes fear, and frankly smiling can be an easy conversation starter.

Ask open-ended questions during networking events.

For example, "Is this your first meeting?" is not an open-ended question because the person will either say "yes" or "no." Instead, how about asking, "So, what brings you to tonight's event?" Want more questions to ask? Here are a dozen:

1. *Who would you most like to meet during this event? Let's go together and introduce ourselves.*

2. *What one or two things would you like to take away from this event?*

3. *What is your area of expertise? Sometimes known as, "So, what do you do for a living?"*

4. *What's the coolest thing that's happened to you all week?*

5. *What is your biggest business or networking challenge and how can I help you?*

6. *What's one of the craziest career situations you've dealt with in your business or profession?*

7. *What is your favorite business or industry publication and why?*

8. *How did you land your current position?*

9. *What was the most important thing you learned when looking for a new position?*

10. *If you had to do it all over again, what would you have done differently in your career and why?*

11. *Which contemporary person do you most admire and why?*

12. *What is one thing no one knows about you?*

Pick your favorites and test them with friends, family, and coworkers. You'll get fun responses, which will make the live gig a lot easier.

Remember, networking is about building relationships – not making the sale – and these questions help break the ice.

Be open to all possibilities and listen carefully for opportunities to make connections.

Networking can take place anywhere, any time.

 MIKE'S STORY

Mike took his dog to the vet. While in the waiting room, he ran into one of his neighbors.

"Hey, how's everything going?" he said. His neighbor replied, "Crappy. We've got this new system and no one knows how to use it."

"Really," Mike said, "I do. Here's how I can help."

He proceeded to provide specific examples of how he solved the very problems his neighbor was having at work.

After listening carefully to these solid examples, his neighbor said, "Hey Mike, you need to come in for an interview. I'll set it up."

Mike was hired and has been happily employed ever since.

Keep in mind the "Rule of Sevens."

Once you begin a conversation, you have seven seconds to make a first impression, 14 seconds to create sufficient interest, and 21 seconds to tell your story. This is why the sound bite you develop in Chapter 5 is so important.

Know you have permission to ask for help.

Think about all the people you have helped over the years, personally and professionally. They certainly would like to help you, remind yourself it's OK to ask for help, you have permission. To get the best results, be clear and specific about the help you need.

COACHING CHALLENGE

Take a deep breath. Exhale. Now, make that call. Send that email. People want to help you. Let them!

PLAY LIST ▶▶ TAKE ACTION!

☒

01.　I have reviewed my previous networking experiences and asked, "Was I begging or building?"

02.　I have tested my networking prowess with people in my comfort zone and am ready to use my new skills at social gatherings and networking events.

03.　I helped several friends make connections this week.

CHAPTER 7
HOW TO REBUILD YOUR NETWORK IN FIVE MINUTES A DAY

Still think networking means a two-hour lunch? Here are ways you can reconnect, rebuild, and maintain your network in five minutes a day. Go ahead, crank up the tunes while you're at it. See if you can take action on one or more of these ideas in two songs or less.

"TAKE FIVE" NETWORKING TIPS

Read The Business Journal during lunch and jot down at least five new contact names each day.

Most large metropolitan cities have The Business Journal publication. Search for your city at www.bizjournals.com. If you're in a small town, you can check the business section of your local newspaper. Movers & Shakers columns are a good source for securing names, titles, promotions, etc.

> A warm referral is always better than a cold lead.

Business profiles help identify companies, names of key players, and more. By the end of the week, you will have 25 new names and/or companies you can target for your career search. Check with your current network to see if they know any of the contact names you identified. A warm referral is always better than a cold lead.

 ## KELLY'S STORY

Kelly claimed she never had time to network or look for a job because she worked in a call center. In her case, the call center monitored her every move. And I do mean "every."

Because of this difficult situation, I recommended she read The Business Journal. She could jot down names of key players on note cards while she ate lunch.

During her lunch, Kelly did read The Business Journal. She took notes, listed names, and researched companies. This strategy was so successful for her that she not only earned an internal promotion — because she was on top of business events, but she ultimately left the employer and landed with a new company she learned about through The Business Journal.

She told me that during her first interview, the company favorably commented on her knowledge about their organization.

They asked her ,"How do you know so much about us?"

She replied, "I read about your firm in <u>The Business Journal</u>. It was a great piece." She then commented on a couple items in the article and shared how she could be a key contributor to the organization.

Kelly was hired.

Send your praises.

Take a few minutes and send a congratulatory note to people in your network. You saw their promotion in the business section, congratulate them!

Provide a genuine compliment.

"Nice shoes," is OK. Better is, "Diane, great post on the e-forum. I really liked the thoughtful way you addressed the issue of the "best of" list. You turned the negative direction to a positive and provided some great tips to help other members get on the list."

Notice how this compliment is specific, rather than general, pointing to a specific action Diane took and how the writer felt about it.

Combine networking with things you already do.

Take five minutes before activities to rehearse your new sound bite, and, if it's an event, plan who you'd like to speak with and why. If it's your first event, sometimes you can get a roster of attendees or at least a list of speakers. If you're in line at the grocery store, instead of reading *The Enquirer* headline, network. If you're at a child's soccer game, network with fellow parents.

One graphic designer joined her neighborhood association and volunteered for a few projects, including designing the association's logo. After getting rave reviews for her work, she soon landed paid projects for local business owners who were also members of this association.

Send thank-you notes.

An attitude of gratitude goes a long way in rebuilding your network.

Let them know you're The Expert.

If you're an industry expert who's written articles, now's the time to repurpose them! Send your articles to all of your clients, family, friends, and prospects. You can do the same for articles written about you.

Put links to the articles on your personal website. If you haven't registered your name as a domain name, do so! Create a visual resume. This helps solidify that you are The Expert everyone should work with — and of course it also helps keep you in touch with your network.

BOB'S STORY

Bob attended a personal branding presentation I conducted for the Association for Women in Communications. Yes, they opened attendance to all for this program, wasn't that terrific? After the presentation, Bob asked me some questions. I saw his business card and recognized his name.

"Aren't you the same Bob I read about in the paper? You had some great tips for job seekers," I said.

"Yes, that was me!" he said.

I told him it was a great piece and that it really demonstrated the one secret necessary to have your network there for you when you need it. "You've got to fuel it to fire it up." It also showed he was an advocate for the community. I mentioned that this article would be a great tool for him to use during his job search. That and his new tag line: "The Likable Engineer."

Here's Bob's story in his own words:

Just wanted to drop you a note and let you know I successfully landed a position as a Project Manager. It is a great fit and I am looking forward to starting my new position. I wish to thank you again for the chat we had after your branding workshop and the advice you provided me. I have received many positive comments on my tag line "The Likeable Engineer." I have only received one negative from another engineer, who thought it trite and self-serving, but at least he remembered. OBTW: He's typical engineer that can't get out of his comfort zone and network.

I often get asked, "What did I learn in the process?"

1) I learned I am in sales and marketing, selling MY value proposition.

2) I learned language is so important. It's not "I think I can do the job," it's "I know I can do the job." Think, can, and maybe where appropriate are replaced with know, will, and absolutely.

3) I discovered in myself a real desire to help others through this process. I will continue to provide support where I can through 40Plus and other venues to coach and mentor. I have learned too much to bury it in the sand. It continues to make me wonder what else God has planned for me.

Did you notice Bob's "fuel it to fire it up" philosophy throughout his job search process? Even though he himself was looking for a job, he was still willing to help others. Congratulations Bob!

COACHING CHALLENGE

Make a list of all your memberships. Are there some networking opportunities coming up in the next week or so? If so, make the most of them.

⊠

01. Make your "Think Big" Network list (Chapter 3).

02. Read <u>The Business Journal</u> during lunch. Jot down the key players' names, titles, and employers. Ask your network if they know any of these key players.

03. After work, send your sound bite to those in your network.

04. Send five people you know an article relevant to their interest. Or email web links to articles.

05. Send a quick thank-you note to someone who's helped you.

06. Congratulate someone.

07. Take five minutes and _____. Be creative and fill in the blank. What's one more thing you can do in five minutes to rebuild your network?

CHAPTER 8
HOW TO CHOOSE THE RIGHT CROWD

One of my favorite festivals here in Milwaukee, WI is the world's largest music festival. There are so many options, 11 days long, 11 stages, and more than 700 bands. They have a great website and an advanced printed program I use to plan out my festival strategy. What days should I go? Who should I go with? What bands should I see? What kind of music do I feel like listening to that day? Do I want to fight the crowds on the most popular days?

The same kinds of thoughts can happen when choosing a new networking group or eliminating one from your current program. Are you hanging with a particular group because it's fun or because its members generate business connections for you? (I must say though, I have landed some great business connections during the festival among peers with common interests like great music!)

SHOULD I STAY OR SHOULD I GO?

Here are some questions to ask yourself about each of your current networking groups and those you are contemplating joining to determine if they are the right group or the wrong crowd:

- Who needs to know about you to help you reach your goals?

- Does this networking organization serve your target audience?

- Does it have members who are your audience — people who know or serve your industry or company targets? If not, it's probably not the group for you.

- How much time does membership in each group take?

- How often do they meet?

- How big is your personal commitment? If a group is not working for you, it's OK to cancel your membership. However, it's not OK to break ties with those people in the group you enjoy most.

PICK THREE!

What groups should you join? Join at least three types of groups.

- **Peer group** for brainstorming, education, and commiserating;

- **Prospects**: A group that is your ideal target market or knows your ideal target market. This group will have people who know an employee of or may directly work for your target companies or those whose business or industry serves your target companies;

- **Professional business group**: Hiring decision-makers often Google your name before meeting with you. Membership in a professional organization can boost your online presence.

After you decide upon your three groups, you'll need to know when a group's a great fit for your career – and when it is not. With some groups you'll know after the first meeting it's not a good fit; others take time to gel. For example, if you're active in the group and meeting the right people, it may be a good fit. The goal is not to collect business cards; the goal is to build relationships that grow with you, your career, and your business. It comes down to this, if you are not building relationships in the group, and you're just going for the food, it's not a good fit.

> **If you are not building relationships in the group, and you're just going for the food, it's not a good fit.**

HOW TO KNOW WHEN IT'S THE WRONG CROWD

If you think you joined the wrong crowd, but are having a hard time deciding which group to dump, it could be like that one-hit-wonder CD you have from the 80's. You have it and you've been storing it all that time for that one song you can now download to your iPod® or MP3 player.

You need to decide if all that time spent with a particular group is worth it. You may want to dump your yearlong membership and show up as an occasional guest.

If you're in a group just to have fun or brainstorm ideas, that's OK. Know that "fun" is the purpose of this particular group. You can still get great referrals to companies where you'd like to work from fun groups. (I'm walking on sunshine...)

Review all of your networking organizations and your individual connections. Identify your key contacts and how you plan to connect with them at least 10 to 14 times a year. Yes, emails, phone calls, and cards count as connections. Lesser contacts can be communicated with three to five times per year.

Finally, if you're staring at a business card like a phone number on an old paper napkin and you can't remember who the heck that person is, that person is no longer a viable contact. Remove them from your networking dance card.

COACHING CHALLENGE

- Determine the groups you'd like to join. Pick three.

- Here are some sample groups:

    Business Network International (BNI):
    www.bni.com

    American Staffing Association:
    www.americanstaffing.net

    National Association for Women Business
    Owners: www.nawbo.org

    Association for Women in Communication:
    www.womcom.org

    National Speakers Association:
    www.nsaspeaker.org

    And of course you can still choose your local
    Parent Teacher Association, Rotary Club,
    Lion's Club, charity, neighborhood association,
    and more.

- Remember to pick three that represent your peer, prospect,
  and professional goals for your career, industry, and
  company targets.

☒

01.   I joined professional organizations
      relevant to my targeted position
      and target companies.

02.   I volunteered for a committee with one
      of my professional organizations.

03.   I set up dance card meetings with at
      least three cool people in my new
      group. This is a meeting outside the
      regular group meetings where you
      learn about each other's business or
      career goals, ideal clients, and more.

04.   I reviewed all the business cards I had
      laying around. For business cards I did
      not recognize, I threw out the card.

05.   I updated my contact database with all
      my new connections, including at least
      one interesting thing I learned about
      each person and where I met him or her.

CHAPTER 9
GET THE MOST FROM EVENTS, PROFESSIONAL GROUPS, AND SOCIAL GATHERINGS

SOCIAL GATHERINGS

Did I hear party? Fantastic! Already I'm starting to relax. And, that's just what happens at parties and other social gatherings. People are more relaxed and receptive to learning more about you. (Better have that Chapter 5 sound bite ready to roll.) They get to know you on a more personal level than simply on a work level. You don't party with your co-workers; you party with your friends, right?

When you're with friends, it's always a good idea to focus on their needs first.

> Listen for opportunities, problems or situations where you may be of service to your friends.

What works best in identifying their needs? Listening. Listen for opportunities, problems or situations where you may be of service to your friends. Helping them solve their problem could turn into a nice opportunity for you. If you can't help, refer your friend to a person in your network who can.

 ## MIC'S STORY

Mic, an electrical engineer, was visiting a friend during Thanksgiving. His friend was just hired at a software company and invited Mic for a tour. Next thing Mic knew, he was meeting the owners who happened to be walking around the office during the tour. Mic landed an interview. The interview was much more relaxing than a traditional interview grilling because the interviewers had more time to spend due to the holiday shut down. He got the job.

Moral: You don't know where your next opportunity will come from. Be flexible and accept those invitations. Someone may be there who could help you land you your next big gig!

BUSINESS FUNCTIONS OR PROFESSIONAL ORGANIZATIONS

Ah the business function. One can only eat so many donuts. However, you've got to go. Not only is it a good strategy politically, but attending helps you get noticed in a positive way. This doesn't mean schmooze or be fake; it does mean let your light shine. Be professional.

HOW TO PARTY LIKE A ROCK STAR

Some pointers before, during, and after you attend an event:

Dress the part.

As one staffing executive told me, "Dress for the job you want, not the job you have." The same thing goes for attending business functions and professional networking events.

Have goals.

Who do you wish to meet at this event? Who needs to know about you? How many new people do you wish to meet? (I recommend meeting at least three new people at each event.) Plan ahead to ensure you connect and meet your networking goals.

Wear a name badge that can be read 15 feet away.

Sounds odd? People will be intrigued and come to meet you and ask you questions. A great opportunity to inspire a connection.

Shy? Bring a friend.

It's much easier to introduce your friend first and then yourself. If this is a work party or function, sit by at least one person you know — and several others you don't. Your goal is to make new connections and learn about other colleagues.

Get a business card.

Jot down at least one unusual or interesting thing you learned about each of the new people you meet on the back of each person's business card. Also list the date and name of the event where you met.

Follow up.

On the back of the business card, list the action you plan to take to follow up with your new connection. For example, you promised the person you'd send them an article on the topic you just discussed, do it!

COACHING CHALLENGE

Be open to and accept invitations to social gatherings and business functions. Plan your networking strategy ahead of time, and plan to meet at least three new people. If you're shy, team up with a friend.

⊠

01.   I said YES to one or more
      social gatherings or business
      functions this month.

02.   I planned ahead and decided
      upon my goal for each event.

03.   I used my new sound bite with confidence
      and people said, "Tell me more!"

04.   I snagged business cards and
      jotted down additional information
      about each person I met.

05.   I entered the new contacts into my
      database and included my notes.

06.   I followed up on any promises I
      made to these new connections.

CHAPTER 10
HOW TO REMEMBER NAMES

One of your favorite tunes just popped up on your car radio. You're singing along loudly. But you cannot for the life of you remember who sings that song, and it is driving you nuts.

ALL YOU'RE TRYING TO REMEMBER IS A NAME.

The same thing can happen at networking events. You remember her face, you think, but the name escapes you. And, she is not wearing a name tag either. Shoot!

What's in a name? It's the one word that's music to your listener's ears. If you're great with faces but have a tough time remembering names. Here are some tips:

INTRODUCE yourself first.

Use your first and last name. The person you're connecting with is probably having a tough time remembering your name as well and introducing yourself first will put him at ease.

LISTEN well.

You've given him your name, now it's time to remember his. Listen for it. The reason most of us immediately forget others' names is that we weren't really paying attention in the first place.

For example, "Hi! I'm Wendy Terwelp, nice to meet you. And you are?"

"I'm Bob Smith, likewise," says Bob.

REPEAT the name immediately.

Repeat it aloud if you are actually meeting someone, such as "Bob Smith? Great! What do you do for a living, Bob?" Do not over-repeat. I once went to a networking event and someone must have heard this tip. I think he said my name at least three or four times in a short amount of time.

It sounded like this, "Wendy, great to meet you Wendy. How's everything going, Wendy?"

I thought to myself, "Now that was a bit over the top."

If you're in a meeting at which everyone is introducing themselves, repeat the name to yourself silently.

ANCHOR the name by attaching a physical action.

A firm handshake is perfect if the interaction is personal, but if you are simply listening to a round of introductions, spell out the person's name with the forefinger of your writing hand in the palm of your other hand as you mentally repeat the name to yourself.

During meetings, I'm a big note taker, so I like to write down people's names if I am at a group meeting or listening to a teleseminar. Writing the name helps me remember, plus I also take a note or two about the person, what they do (if it's mentioned), what company they work for, and so on. This helps me reconnect with them later.

"Bob, great to see you again. How's everything going for you at ACME?"

REVIEW all the names.

Mentally recall each new person during introductions. If there are more than about 20 people, keep reviewing the most recent 20 people's names as the introductions continue. If you are interacting with one person, use that person's name several times, but don't be too obvious.

One great technique is to introduce that person to others. You can say something like, "Bob, have you met Janet? Janet, this is Bob Smith."

ASSOCIATE the names.

Alliteration is especially helpful for large groups or if more than one person has the same first name. Barbara in blue, Mary the mortgage broker, or Frank the financial planner can help you remember who is who.

At one networking event, we actually went around the group and introduced ourselves by saying one or two words that described us, followed by our name. I still remember "Calling Card Candy" who sold telephone calling cards.

LEARN something unique or special about this person.

During your brief conversation you may discover interesting facts. Put this on the back of the person's business card. For example, Mary speaks seven languages. Ramona used to be a professional juggler!

FOLLOW UP.

If you make promises to others during your networking event or meeting it is important to follow up promptly. If you promised to send them an article on their topic of interest, jot that down on their business card — then do it the next day.

COACHING CHALLENGE

Time to test out your "remembering names" techniques. Schedule your next networking event and use the tips to ensure you remember attendees' names for fast and easy follow up.

▸▸ TAKE ACTION!

⊠

01. When you get home from your next meeting, jot down the names of the people you met. Yes, you've got their card, but writing the name helps people remember it.

02. Send each person you met a quick email. Thank them and follow up with anything you promised to do during the event.

03. Update your contact management system with the new connections, including your association word, the unique thing you learned, where you met, and the date you met the person.

CHAPTER 11
FAST & EASY WAYS TO FOLLOW UP

You've got their card, now what? You entered their information into your database, now what? How do you manage it all without going crazy and using up all your time? Here's how:

SEVEN TIPS TO CRANK UP YOUR FOLLOW-UP

Schedule it.

Schedule a regular time every week (or daily) to follow up with your current and new contacts. Select at least five contacts per week to connect with; that's only one contact per day during a workweek.

Pick a method.

Determine what method you will use to follow up with your network. Methods can include: mass emails (e-zines, group updates), cards, phone calls or in-person visits. Then, take action.

Send an article of interest.

You're already reading the trade and business media, send an article that relates to one of your connection's interests.

 JACK'S STORY

One day I opened the door to my office and stepped on a news article about employment issues. I picked it up and saw that it had come from Jack, a business owner in my office complex. It was a good article.

I walked down to his office and thanked him for it.

"Thanks, Jack. That article was dead on, and I'm going to pass it along to my clients. What made you think of it?" I said.

He replied, "Well, it's something I do. I read so many newspapers and magazines that when I find something I think will interest one of my friends or clients, I send it along. That way when someone needs an appraisal, they think of me first."

"Cool! Mind if I pass on your idea to my job seekers? I think they could use this strategy to stay in touch with their networks!" I said.

He loved it and said I could pass it on.

Moral: You want people to remember you when they need your services so they refer you. This helps ensure your network is there when you need it. "You've got to fuel your network to fire it up."

You can also email related websites or articles. Like your own articles or those written about you!

This is a regular practice of mine with clients, colleagues, and friends. Because the articles are relevant to their careers, it's not considered spam.

Send a card.

Stand out from the crowd and send a card on an unexpected holiday, like Groundhog's Day.

 ## STEVE'S STORY

Steve called me up one day to tell me his latest, a new job, higher level position, six-figure salary, bonus, and a car. Not too shabby.

"How'd you land this latest gig," I asked.

"Well you know me I'm all about networking, like you said. But here's a new twist I use, feel free to pass it on," he said. What was the twist? "I just send people in my network a card on a weird holiday and let them know where I'm at."

He is so successful with networking that he went from an entry- level sales position to a vice president earning six figures. And, he tells me, he is still getting calls and offers regularly. He now uses this same strategy to drive new business to his latest employer.

What did Steve consider a weird holiday? Ground Hog's Day, St. Patrick's Day, April Fool's Day, and so on — non-traditional holidays. In the cards, he would tell people what he's been up to, his latest position, what he's been doing, what he's looking for now, and personal information. He'd also thank people for their help throughout his career.

Who did he send these cards to? Everyone he knew. Steve had no fear. He'd even send these types of "un-holiday" cards to interviewers who did not hire him.

"Hey, you never know where an opportunity will turn up," was Steve's thought. And it worked.

If you prefer, send an e-card. I use Plaxo, which has a cool birthday tracking feature and an e-card service. It's been terrific touching base with people on their birthdays. I get to hear the latest, and yes, it has led to new business as well as cool success stories. You're reading some of them in this book, and you can see more throughout my website at: www.knocks.com.

Develop a mini-newsletter sent quarterly.

As an industry expert, you're already writing all those articles. Why not reuse them? You've got fans, let them know what you're doing.

Send thank-you notes.

When I was a recruiter (and now too), I always recommended that my candidates send thank-you notes to each interviewer. One candidate, Chris, handwrote his note and faxed it to the company the same day of his interview. Minutes later, I got a call from the company. "We love Chris!" they told me. "Did you know he FAXED us a thank-you note? No one has ever done that before. Heck, we hardly ever get thanked after an interview, much less the same day. Tell Chris he's hired!" And, I did. And, he was.

Be prompt.

Return calls within 24 hours and email new contacts the same day, if possible, with the action you promised when you met the person.

Keep in mind motivational speaker Zig Ziglar's philosophy: "If you help enough people get what they want, you'll get what you want." In other words, fuel your network and your connections will be fired up to help you in return. Again, this is the No. 1 way to ensure your network is there for you when you need it.

COACHING CHALLENGE

Take a look at your schedule. Have you made time to reconnect? If not, get out your calendar now and schedule time to make contact with people in your network this week. I typically use Fridays to do this. Pick a regular day and time and then follow up!

PLAY LIST ▸▸TAKE ACTION!

⊠

01.   I've scheduled a regular time in my calendar to reconnect with my network every week.

02.   I've decided on the ways I wish to communicate with my network.

03.   I made a networking plan and am sticking to it. Use the Networking Action Plan worksheet in Chapter 15.

05.   Use the Staying-in-Touch worksheet in Chapter 15.

CHAPTER 12
MAKE YOUR NETWORK THRIVE

The goal in networking is to build relationships so your network is there for you when you need it. Like a giant mosh pit, you want to know people will catch you when you jump in. In order to do this, you've got to remain connected to make your network thrive. Here are some tips:

Identify your key contacts.

Pinpoint those who need to know about you and develop a plan to connect with them at least 10 to 14 times per year. Yes, emails, phone calls, and cards count as contacts. Others can be contacted three to five times per year.

If you don't remember the person, that person is no longer a viable contact, and you can delete them from your database.

Send an "update" note to contacts regularly.

Your network needs to be up-to-date with the latest news. Your friends, family, clients, and colleagues like to hear about what you're doing. This helps them know more about you. Keep it professional.

Review your networking plan often.

What's working? What's not? Create your very own networking plan by using the worksheet in Chapter 15.

Join or start your own networking group.

Help others network. You can do this through live events, social gatherings, and general introductions. Check out my Rock Your Network® groups on Facebook. I also host live networking events as well.

 ALLY'S STORY

One client, Ally, was downsized from a Fortune 50. Rather than get depressed, Ally took action. She started her own networking group with a positive focus to help other job seekers as well as business owners in the area connect. The group got such positive reviews her story was featured in the business section of a major newspaper.

Know that networking is simply having a conversation with friends.

After conducting a Rock Your Network® event at Brigham Young University in Hawaii, one of the students told me, "Wow, this was easy. I always thought networking was hard. It's not. It's just like having a conversation with friends!"

COACHING CHALLENGE

What have you done for your network lately? Schedule some time to reconnect. A good networker gives to their network and maintains their network.

PLAY LIST ▸▸ **TAKE ACTION!**

⊠

01. I created a networking plan and have taken action.

02. I now send a quarterly update note to friends, family, and colleagues.

03. I've joined some networking groups online and off.

04. I have connected and introduced my friends to each other.

CHAPTER 13
ROCK YOUR NETWORK® ONLINE

In the past, employers used to hire private investigators to do background checks on key personnel. Now, they can quickly Google a person prior to the interview.

With that in mind, here's one tip I mentioned in *The Wall Street Journal*: Google yourself first to see if you have digital dirt. Digital dirt is anything unflattering found about you online. You know, that time you danced on the table at that last party and your friends took pictures of you and put them on MySpace and Facebook. That's something you don't want turning up in a search by potential employers. You want to take control of your reputation online, just like a rock star with a great press agent.

BE YOUR OWN PRESS AGENT

A good press agent puts the spotlight on her client's best brand attributes, preserving her client's good name. Check for your own digital dirt and take control of your online reputation. Google your name and use quotes like this: "Wendy Terwelp."

■ How many total references to your name did you find (number will be in upper right-hand corner)?

- Of the first three pages listed in Google with your name (roughly 30 listings in total), how many of the listings found are actually you?

- Of the references / listings that are you, how many are relevant — and truly reflect who you are, your business, and how you wish to be perceived?

If what you see would embarrass you if your mom or boss found out (the mom or boss test), change it. How? Remove your digital dirt or bury it.

CLEAN UP YOUR REPUTATION

You can remove your dirt by removing unflattering pictures of you dancing on that table. If your friends have a copy on their site, ask them to remove it. If your dirt has gone viral, you'll need to bury it. One of the best tools for burying your dirt is to create a blog. According to Kirsten Dixson, co-author of "Career Distinction," blog stands for "Better Listing On Google." Blogs get higher rankings because content changes regularly. You can also use a blog to demonstrate your thought leadership and reinforce your personal brand.

It's far too easy to uncover the truth. It's much more effective to be yourself. Be authentic.

SOCIAL NETWORKING

Another way to improve your reputation online and improve your networking odds is to join social networking sites.

What sites should you join if you're in job search mode? I recommend LinkedIn, Facebook, Twitter, and Pulse (Plaxo's social networking site). eCademy is another good site if you're in the global market place.

To get the most from your chosen social networking sites, be sure you have a detailed profile that is professional, yet personal. If you wouldn't want your mom or your boss to see it — revise it. Want more help with your profile? Check out my "Bio that Rocks" worksheet on page 108.

Read each site's instructions carefully. Check your privacy settings. Invite only those people whom you know and whom you feel confident in referring to others. Your goal in job search mode is NOT to have one million friends. Your goal is to make real and helpful connections.

Maintain these networks by writing short updates on what you're doing. For Twitter, this means updates no longer than 140 characters.

A tool you can use to cross-post all your social networking updates is ping.fm. It allows you to take five minutes or less and do an update post ONCE. It then posts this update to all your social networks. Their motto: "Ping.fm is a simple service that makes updating your social networks a snap." Hey, a snap is less than five minutes!

Review LinkedIn and Pulse updates sent to your inbox. Send appropriate comments to those in your network who have new jobs, updated their profiles, and shared interesting information.

COACHING CHALLENGE

- Got dirt? Remove it or bury it. Remember, if you'd be embarrassed that your mom or boss saw these items, you've got dirt.

- Next, select your social networking sites.

- Build a dynamic online profile using the template on page 108.

- Start inviting your friends, family, and others whom you trust. Search out work and college alumni if you wish.

- If you're on LinkedIn, ask for recommendations and reciprocate. If you send a recommendation to key players in your network, they'll likely write one for you. This can be a valuable resource for you to use on your resume, your personal website, and on your reference dossier left with interviewers.

- If it's been some time since you've talked with some of your connections, make a call. You can keep this call to five minutes and let him know what you're doing and that you'd like to invite him into your network. People are happy to help.

One of my clients, a CEO, made personal calls to ask people to join his LinkedIn network. One of his contacts, a CEO of another firm, told him to send over his new LinkedIn profile (based on my Bio that Rocks format). My client sent the new bio and landed an interview for the following week. Make the call.

- Use the Online Action Plan on page 106 to keep you motivated online.

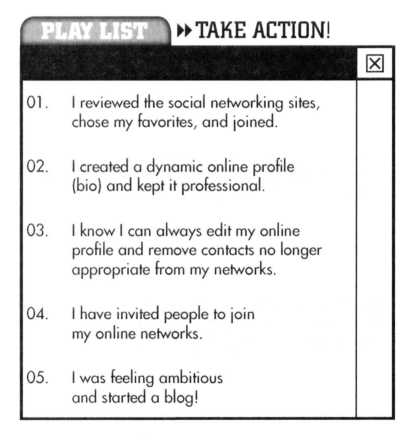

PLAY LIST ▶▶ **TAKE ACTION!**

⊠

01. I reviewed the social networking sites, chose my favorites, and joined.

02. I created a dynamic online profile (bio) and kept it professional.

03. I know I can always edit my online profile and remove contacts no longer appropriate from my networks.

04. I have invited people to join my online networks.

05. I was feeling ambitious and started a blog!

CHAPTER 14
THAT'S A WRAP!

Feel like a rock star networker yet? Here are a few reminders:

Networking is 10 times more effective than posting your resume online or answering job ads.

How are you currently spending your job search time? If you're spraying and praying — that is spraying your resume online and praying someone calls you, rethink your strategy. Allocate the majority of your job search time to networking. Besides, won't it be fun reconnecting and having great conversations with friends? Remember, people want to help you.

Know that face-to-face and voice-to-voice connections are more important.

Don't just solely rely on using online networking tools. People want to feel that personal connection. Personal connections build trust. Trust = referrals. Take action now and set up a quick meeting or phone call.

Networking is a two-way street.

Always asking for favors kills your network. Think about Bob's story, The Likable Engineer, in Chapter 7. He was out of work, yet volunteered for organizations, passed along referrals to those in his network, and gave. This resulted in new connections for him that led to a job. What are some ways you can help those in your network?

15 WAYS TO RECONNECT FIVE MINUTES A DAY

1. **Schedule time to network**; create a networking plan.

2. **Create your own on-brand sound bite** (Chapter 5).

3. Take five minutes and **update your contact list** to see who is in your network. Think BIG.

4. Take five minutes and **throw out business cards** from those you don't remember.

5. Take five minutes and **send an email** to people in your network.

6. Take five minutes and **review your LinkedIn updates**; send a quick email to those in your network who've shared news – like a new job.

7. Take five minutes and **call a friend** just to see how they are doing.

8. **Ask a friend how you can help** him or her.

9. **Send an article** to someone in your network.

10. **Send a link** to a cool website to someone in your network.

11. Take five minutes and **introduce your friends to each other** at the next networking event or party.

12. When you get business cards, jot down the date, name of event, and at least one unique thing you learned about the person so you can follow up with them later.

13. **Follow up** with the action promised.

14. **Send a card** on a weird holiday like Steve on page 65.

15. Take five minutes and **thank** a friend, family member, boss, colleague or coworker.

After reading this book, now you know...

> **the power of the one secret that ensures your network is there for you when you need it: You've got to "fuel your network to fire it up."**

> **that networking can take place anytime, anywhere. Be open to all possibilities.**

> **that networking does not mean a two-hour lunch! Networking CAN take only five minutes a day.**

Are you ready to rock your network? Go for it! I want to hear from you!

Rock on,

CHAPTER 15
ROCK YOUR NETWORK® WORKSHEETS

CHAPTER 3
YOUR CIRCLE OF INFLUENCE
WORKSHEETS

PEOPLE YOU KNOW

Quick Start: List as many personal connections you can think of and write them on the spokes surrounding your name.

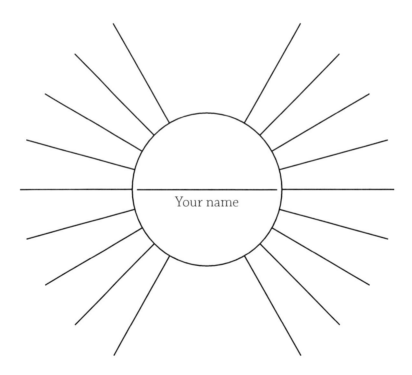

Continue to brainstorm your list by providing family, friends and service professionals. Remember service professionals are people like your hair stylist, dentist, massage therapist, etc. Don't worry about providing phone numbers right now; just list the names.

Family Members

_____

_____

_____

_____

_____

Friends

_____

_____

_____

_____

Service Professionals

_____

_____

_____

_____

PEOPLE RELATED TO YOUR INDUSTRY OR PROFESSION

Quick Start: List as many contacts you can think of who are in your same profession or who serve or supply your industry.

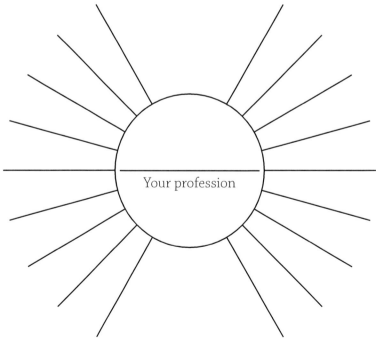

Your profession

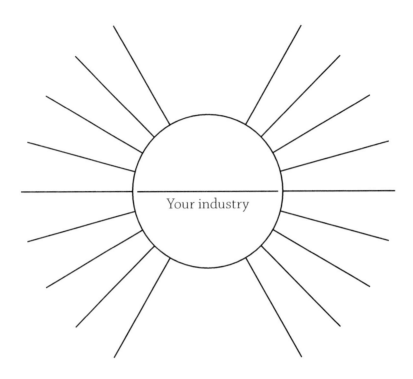

Your industry

Continue to brainstorm your list by providing the names of your customers, colleagues or competitors, and people who serve or supply your industry. Don't worry about providing phone numbers right now; just list the names.

Customers

_____

_____

_____

_____

_____

Colleagues/Competitors

_____

_____

_____

_____

_____

Industry Vendors/Service Providers

_____

_____

_____

_____

CORPORATE CONTACTS

Family Members

Does a family member have a direct connection to a customer, colleague/competitor, or someone who serves or supplies your industry? If your family member doesn't know someone directly, he or she may know someone who knows someone on the inside.

Family Member Name: _____

Customers:_____

Competitors: _____

Industries/Professions: _____

_____

Family Member Name: _____

Customers:_____

Competitors: _____

Industries/Professions: _____

_____

Family Member Name: _____

Customers:_____

Competitors: _____

Industries/Professions: _____

_____

Family Member Name: _____

Customers:_____

Competitors: _____

Industries/Professions: _____

_____

Family Member Name: _____

Customers:_____

Competitors: _____

Industries/Professions: _____

Friends

Does a friend have a direct connection to a customer, colleague/competitor, or someone who serves or supplies your industry? If your friend doesn't know someone directly, he or she may know someone who knows someone on the inside.

Friend's Name:_____

Customers:_____

Competitors: _____

Industries/Professions: _____

_____

Friend's Name:_____

Customers:_____

Competitors: _____

Industries/Professions: _____

_____

Friend's Name:_____

Customers:_____

Competitors: _____

Industries/Professions: _____

_____

Friend's Name:_____

Customers:_____

Competitors: _____

Industries/Professions: _____

_____

Friend's Name:_____

Customers:_____

Competitors: _____

Industries/Professions: _____

_____

Service professionals

Does your contact have a direct connection to a customer, colleague/competitor, or someone who serves or supplies your industry? If your he or she doesn't know someone directly, he or she may know someone who knows someone on the inside.

Professional's Name: _____

Customers: _____

Competitors: _____

Industries/Professions: _____

_____

Professional's Name: _____

Customers: _____

Competitors: _____

Industries/Professions: _____

_____

Professional's Name: _____

Customers:_____

Competitors: _____

Industries/Professions: _____

_____

Professional's Name: _____

Customers:_____

Competitors: _____

Industries/Professions: _____

_____

Professional's Name: _____

Customers:_____

Competitors: _____

Industries/Professions: _____

_____

Extended family, friends, co-workers

Does your third cousin's brother-in-law have a direct connection to a customer, colleague/competitor, or someone who serves or supplies your industry? Dig deep into your connections and see if your acquaintances know someone directly or know someone who knows someone on the inside.

Acquaintance's Name: _____

Customers:_____

Competitors: _____

Industries/Professions: _____

_____

Acquaintance's Name: _____

Customers:_____

Competitors: _____

Industries/Professions: _____

_____

Acquaintance's Name: _____

Customers:_____

Competitors: _____

Industries/Professions: _____

Acquaintance's Name: _____

Customers:_____

Competitors: _____

Industries/Professions: _____

_____

Acquaintance's Name: _____

Customers:_____

Competitors: _____

Industries/Professions: _____

_____

CHAPTER 5
ROCK YOUR NETWORK®
THREE-STEP SYSTEM
WORKSHEET

STEP ONE: FOCUS

The specific job I am seeking is:

_____

_____

_____

STEP TWO: SHARE

The bottom-line value I bring to the table is:

_____

_____

_____

STEP THREE: **TELL**

Who do you know who knows someone at:

_____

_____

_____

NEW SOUND BITE

_____

_____

_____

_____

_____

_____

CHAPTER 7
CRANK UP YOUR
FOLLOW-UP CHECK LIST

☐ I set up a regular time every week to fuel my network by following up.

☐ I determined the best way to follow up with each person in my network. Strategies I plan to use include:

_____

_____

_____

☐ I sent articles of interest to _____ people this week.

☐ I sent _____ cards to _____ people this week.

☐ I started a min-newsletter and plan to send the first issue on _____ (specific date); this newsletter is quarterly.

☐ I sent a thank-you note or email to _____ people this week.

☐ I used Twitter to update my network in a professional manner.

☐ I updated my status on LinkedIn in a professional, positive manner.

☐ I scheduled time to call _____ people in my network just to enlighten their day and provide help, if needed.

☐ I scheduled _____ one-on-one meetings this week to reconnect with my network and learn more about each person.

Notes:

_____

_____

_____

_____

_____

_____

_____

_____

_____

CHAPTER 9
GET THE MOST FROM
EVENTS CHECKLIST

☐ I rehearsed my sound bite from Chapter 5 and
I am ready to roll!

☐ I set my networking goals for this event. They are:

_____

_____

_____

_____

☐ I have at least three open-ended questions in my arsenal.
They are:

_____

_____

_____

_____

- ☐ I am dressed for the job I want.

- ☐ I am bringing a friend.

- ☐ I'll wear a name tag that can be read from 15 feet away.

- ☐ I will listen for opportunities of how I can help others.

- ☐ I will learn about other people's professions and businesses by asking open-ended questions.

- ☐ I will fuel the network to fire it up by focusing on building relationships, not making the sale or asking for a job.

- ☐ I'll arrive early to network and meet new people.

- ☐ I'll stay late to continue building positive business relationships.

- ☐ I will get business cards.

- ☐ I will jot down the name of the event, the date, and something I learn on the back of the business card I receive from each person I meet.

- ☐ I will follow up on any action I promised the following day.

- ☐ Once I learn of opportunities to participate in this professional organization, I will take an active role and join a committee or take on a leadership position.

- ☐ I am open to all possibilities. I know opportunities can happen any time, anywhere!

CHAPTER 11
NETWORKING ACTION PLAN

By writing down your networking goals, you commit to them and take action.

Goals   COMPLETION DATE

Sample: *Toss old business cards*   *01/01/10*

_____

_____

_____

_____

Join Networking Groups
GROUP   JOIN BY (DATE)
Sample: *Attend Association of Women in*
Communication meeting   *01/01/10*

_____

_____

_____

_____

Attend Events

Select and commit to attend the following events with each group. Pick major events so you get a chance to network with more people:

Group: _____

Event: _____

Date of Event: _____

Group: _____

Event: _____

Date of Event: _____

Group: _____

Event: _____

Date of Event: _____

Group: _____

Event: _____

Date of Event: _____

Group: _____

Event: _____

Date of Event: _____

Update your Contact Management Database (Outlook, Act!, Plaxo, etc.)

By (date): _____

Set up Network Database

By (date): _____

Populate Network Database with your contacts

By (date): _____

Create system to keep network up-to-date

By (date): _____

CHAPTER 11
STAYING-IN-TOUCH WORKSHEET

Remember in Chapter 11, we talked about how to make your network thrive by staying in touch with your contacts. Use this sheet to set your connection goals.

Name: _____

When to Stay-in-Touch: _____

Way to Stay-in-Touch: _____

_____

☐ Done

Name: _____

When to Stay-in-Touch: _____

Way to Stay-in-Touch: _____

_____

☐ Done

Name: _____

When to Stay-in-Touch: _____

Way to Stay-in-Touch: _____

_____

☐ Done

Name: _____

When to Stay-in-Touch: _____

Way to Stay-in-Touch: _____

_____

☐ Done

Name: _____

When to Stay-in-Touch: _____

Way to Stay-in-Touch: _____

_____

☐ Done

Name: _____

When to Stay-in-Touch: _____

Way to Stay-in-Touch: _____

_____

☐ Done

Name: _____

When to Stay-in-Touch: _____

Way to Stay-in-Touch: _____

_____

☐ Done

Name: _____

When to Stay-in-Touch: _____

Way to Stay-in-Touch: _____

_____

☐ Done

CHAPTER 13
ONLINE ACTION STEPS

Review other people's bios online including colleagues, competitors, favorite authors, actors, business professionals, etc. Whose do you like?

_____

_____

Don't like? Why?

_____

_____

_____

Whose bio has ideas you can integrate into your own bio?

_____

_____

_____

Use the "Bio that Rocks" template on page 108 and write (or rewrite) your bio.

Update your bio page in the various online networks you have joined. ☐ Done

Review your "about us" page on your own website or LinkedIn profile. Does this page fit your brand and your new bio criteria? If not, what changes need to be made?

_____

_____

_____

_____

Review the list of contacts you developed. Now that you have criteria for those you wish to invite to your network – who fits?

Who does not?

_____

_____

_____

Invite those who do. ☐ Done

CHAPTER 13
BIO THAT ROCKS WORKSHEET

Brand statement / tagline / elevator speech:

_____

_____

_____

_____

Your niche / target market:

_____

_____

What you do / process:

_____

_____

_____

Benefit(s) people get when they work with you:

_____

_____

_____

Specialty areas (offerings):

_____

_____

_____

_____

_____

Tags, areas of interest, brand attributes:

_____

_____

TAKE ACTION! WORKSHEET

List the top three things you'll do this week to rebuild your network.

My first action step this week is:

_____

_____

_____

My second action step this week is:

_____

_____

_____

My third action step this week is:

_____

_____

_____

TOP THREE TAKEAWAYS
WORKSHEET

My first biggest takeaway from reading this book is:

_____

_____

_____

My second biggest takeaway from reading this book is:

_____

_____

_____

My third biggest takeaway from reading this book is:

_____

_____

_____

CHAPTER 16
NETWORKING RESOURCES FOR ROCK STARS

OPPORTUNITY KNOCKS™ ONLINE RESOURCES

Seven Secrets of Networking

In this self-study course, I provide you with the answers to help you choose the right networking group, start a conversation, and more. Order this self-study program here: www.knocks.com/Programs/NetworkingSecrets.html

Rock Your Network® Online: How to Get the Most from LinkedIn and Other Social Networking Tools

Did you know employers Google you before ever meeting you? With this in mind, it's imperative you know your online reputation. This program helps you build a positive reputation online and teaches you how to get the most from social networking sites.

Your investment in this comprehensive 5-week program gives you the inside scoop on getting the most from LinkedIn and other social networks. I guide you every step of the way using exercises, worksheets, and audio.

The CEO mentioned in Chapter 13 blazed through this program and reconnected with another CEO who asked him for an interview.

You can get these results too. This program provides you with all the tools you need to improve your online presence and rock your network using sites like LinkedIn! You also learn about little known FREE sites that pack a lot of punch and improve your online reputation. Order this intense program here: www.knocks.com/RYN/Social_Networking_Course.html

Rock Your Network® — the audio

I help you take your holiday networking to the next level with fast and easy ways to follow up, how to get the most from your connections the right way, and how to make the most of holiday festivities. Order this self-study program here: www.knocks.com/RYN/Rockyournetworkteleclass.html

Rock Your Network® Events

Check out the Events Page for my next gig: www.knocks.com/Events/Calendar.html

Self-Study Programs

Check out the self-study page to get audio recordings of radio shows, teleseminars, and MORE:

www.knocks.com/Programs/Career_Programs.html

RESOURCES FOR NETWORKING STATISTICS

1. "Post Your Resume Online – With Caution," Matt Krumrie, Star Tribune Sales and Marketing, Dec. 8, 2008 http://tinyurl.com/qvnx9j

2. *Executive Job Market Intelligence Report 2009* http://www.execunet.com/e_trends_survey.cfm

3. CareerXroads 8th Annual Source of Hire Study: *What Happened in 2008 and What It Means for 2009*, Gerry Crispin, SPHR and Mark Mehler, Feb. 2009.

4. "Upside of Holiday Work," Anna Prior, The Wall Street Journal, *Starting Out*, Dec. 21, 2008.

EXPERIENCE
WENDY TERWELP
LIVE!

Wendy J. Terwelp is available for speaking gigs, workshops, association events, and individual and/or group coaching nationwide. If you wish to hire her, please connect directly:

Wendy J. Terwelp
c/o Opportunity Knocks
11431 N. Port Washington Rd.
Suite 101
Mequon, WI 53092

Phone: 262.241.4655

Email: consultant@knocks.com

Web: www.knocks.com

Want to order more copies for you and your network?
ORDER HERE!

Want more? *Ask about our quantity discount!*

Check one: ☐ **$20** printed book
☐ **$15** e-book in PDF format
(email address required)

Name: _____

Billing Address: _____

_____

Phone: _____

Email:_____

Payment due in advance: Visa, Discover, MasterCard, and American Express accepted.

Card # _____

CVV Number: _____ Exp. date: _____
(Number on back of card by your signature.)

Signed:_____

Date: _____

Make checks payable to:
Opportunity Knocks, 11431 N. Port Washington Rd.,
Suite 101, Mequon, WI 53092